THE
Archive Photographs
SERIES
EASTON

My grandmother, Jane Ellery, and auntie Kath (Kathleen Ellery) in the garden of No. 39 St Mark's Road in 1942.

THE
Archive Photographs
SERIES

EASTON

Compiled by
Veronica Smith

CHALFORD

First published 1998
Copyright © Veronica Smith, 1998

The Chalford Publishing Company
St Mary's Mill, Chalford,
Stroud, Gloucestershire, GL6 8NX

ISBN 0 7524 1092 X

Typesetting and origination by
The Chalford Publishing Company
Printed in Great Britain by
Bailey Print, Dursley, Gloucestershire

Contents

Foreword   6

Introduction   7

Acknowledgements   8

1. Greenbank   9

2. Eastville   21

3. St Mark's Church and Environs   35

4. Baptist Mills to Stapleton Road   55

5. Stapleton Road   69

6. St Gabriel's and Thereabouts   83

7. Easton Road to Roman Road   103

Foreword

by David Harrison of the *Bristol Evening Post*

George Orwell, unerring observer of the British, summed it all up pretty well. 'Before the war', he wrote in *Coming Up for Air*, 'it was summer all the year round.' Frank Norman put it more simply in a hit musical about changes in ordinary communities: 'Fings', he suggested, 'ain't what they used t'be.' And even Beatle Paul McCartney admitted that it was yesterday that 'all my troubles seemed so far away'.

There's a lovely piece of uncredited graffiti which reads: 'Nostalgia isn't what is used to be.' Was it ever? Wasn't it always summer when we were young? And didn't the green fields stretch away to the horizon, full of daisies and buttercups to make flower chains, and trees laden with sour crab apples and conkers for the taking? Probably not, but then nostalgia ain't what it used to be...

Those of us who write about history and nostalgia know all about the 'green fields syndrome' – you know, the old codgers who look at a housing development and say, sadly, 'I remember when this was all fields.' It's a cousin to the 'unlocked doors syndrome' – 'We never locked our front doors in the old days' – and the more famous 'rose-coloured glasses syndrome' which maintains that 'things were all so much better in the Good Old Days'. Gilbert and Sullivan's *Mikado* had a special punishment for those who yearned for every century and every country but their own, which seems a bit hard – after all, we all do it sometimes. That's the other one, the 'grass is always greener on the other side of the hill syndrome'.

Books like this one are a valuable, no an invaluable, contribution to our understanding of the past. These are frozen moments in time, landscapes, and people that belong to another world which some of us might remember and others are keen to learn about. We can look at places like Easton today and, with the help of this book, imagine how it was before the Second World War and before the circuit road stabbed it through the heart. That's not 'green fields syndrome', that's a healthy interest in our past, in the characters that made us what we are today. Without a past, it is impossible to understand the present and God knows we all need to do that to survive in a bewildering world.

Personally, I have learned more about Easton from Veronica Smith's evocative books than from any number of stuffy histories. Books like this aren't museum pieces, frozen moments in time, agreed, but just look at what they so lovingly preserve. The much-loved old pub, the fleeting smile on the face of a child who might not have had much to smile about, the kind of neighbours always remembered with affection, the shopkeepers who knew their customers and their problems and often helped in whatever way they could. There are eccentrics here and the kind of special characters that every neighbourhood has – and ordinary, anonymous citizens going about their daily chores. You don't have to have known them to share a brief second or two of their lives before they move off the stage. This is not the kind of history that chronicles the destiny of a nation or the toppling of an empire, but it is far more real to everyone than yet another battlefield or political treaty. This is REAL.

Veronica is one of a number of community historians preserving vital memories of ordinary people so that their children and grandchildren can gain an understanding of what they were like and how their home territories have changed. It is important work, and this is the kind of book that will itself be lovingly preserved and carefully pored over by generations to come, for whom our present will be their rose-coloured past. Nostalgia isn't what it used to be... is it?

Introduction

Since the publication of *Erstwhile Easton* in December 1996, I have amassed a further collection of photographs, many from kind readers and others from Mike Tozer, Crockerne Photographs, Pill, who every now and then will pop a little gem in the post to me, knowing it will receive a rapturous response. It is, therefore, most exciting to be able to present these fascinating pictures to the reading public, courtesy of the Chalford Publishing Company. In truth, I regard it as a great honour to work with a publisher whose local history books are of such a high standard.

I should like to take this opportunity to thank everyone who has helped me with background information and those who have delved indefatigably and nagged others to raid their attics for forgotten photographs and, furthermore, dredged up names from years past. Without the hard work you have all put in on my behalf, this book would not have been possible. You have my undying gratitude.

Acknowledgements

I should like to thank the following for providing photographs and information:

Ashman's, Jenny Bell, John Bennett, Ben Bird, Mr Bishop, Les and Rosa Brewer, Bristol Evening Post, Bristol Sweet Mart, Clive Bryant (City Line), Jack Bryer, Barbara Bulman, David Cheesley, Trina Clarke, Audrey Cook, Grace Cooper, Doreen Cowley, Jean and Roy Cowley, Mrs Crew, R. Crowcombe, Mr Cunningham, Colin Downs, Colin and Mary Floyde, Lewis Fox, Pamela Fursman, Doris Harrington, Marlene Holloway, Alice Howard, Doreen Howarth, Norman Irwin, Mrs E. James, Dennis Lealan, Molly Maby, D. Mansfield, Hilary May, James Merrett, Clive Oliver, Dave Packer, Barbara Payne, Jack and Olive Payne, Mike Purnell, Charlie Randall, Doreen Redmore, Ralph Robbins, Ern Shepherd, Brenda Smallridge, John Smele, John Stone, Bob Stubbins, Muriel Taylor, Ilene Timbrell, Mike Tozer, Hilda Ward, Iris Warn, Adrian Warrington, Ivy Wilcox.

One
Greenbank

We begin our Easton excursion on the perimeter of the district with a look at the elegantly structured Rose Green School, long since demolished, but once the stepping stone to secretarial skills which enabled many local girls to attain prestigious office jobs.

From Rose Green School could be viewed the tall redbrick building which housed Packer's chocolate manufacturing business; one of their vehicles is seen here being collected from W.J. Bence & Sons, coachbuilders and wheelwrights of Longwell Green. Packer's later amalgamated with Carsons of Shortwood and underwent several changes of ownership before its present incarnation as 'Leaf Industries'.

Packer's Fire Brigade at the Warmley Fire Brigade Tournament in 1921. From left to right, back row: Vernon Crane, Mr Hamby, -?-, -?-, Hugh Clare, Mr Crawford, Bill Shepherd, -?-. The two men identified in the middle of the front row are Mr Deacon and Mr Leaman (or Lemmon).

Packer's factory was bordered on one side by Carlyle Road and it is here we come upon a Coronation party in full swing in 1953. The picture was loaned by Mrs Hill who still lives in the street.

And so to Greenbank Road where one might have once paused to buy a quarter of corned beef or ham at Lusty's grocery store on the corner of Hinton Road. This is now the Spar and the side door and window are blocked up – a sad reflection on the prevalence of crime in today's society.

The sound of children's voices calling across the playground leads us over to Greenbank School. Here two classes from the 1950s pose with their teachers. The first group (*above*), pictured in May 1958, are in the charge of Mrs Anthony. The little blonde boy on the right, proudly sporting wellington boots, is seemingly hoping for some puddles through which to splash. John Hoffman, whose aunt, Iris Warn, loaned the photograph, is second from left, front row. *Below*: Mrs Nicholas's class in May 1959. She is sitting next to John Hoffman, who had great rapport with her. These were the days when the Co-op still flourished on the corner of Hinton Road.

A musical interlude at the school, 1930s. The girl with ringlets conducting the 'orchestra' is Pat Drew. Among the children are John Williams, Richard Dyer, Jean Gingell, and Jean Uren.

Close by the school, but far back in time, to a funeral procession wending its way to the cemetery. The picture would seem to date from the first decade of this century but who was Fireman Smith and what brave action merited the posthumous honour of this magnificent entourage?

A peaceful turn of the century Daisy Road comes into view. The absence of traffic, save for an occasional horse and cart, enables children to play freely in the street.

A swift visit to Bruce Road to look again upon the Kings Arms before it was converted into a private dwelling and the lovely gothic window vanished for ever. Alas, no longer are 'Parties Catered For'.

Down to Tudor Road Methodist church where we catch the children just about to tuck into some party treats in 1946. The girl at the table to the left, moving out of focus, is Jean Uren, with her friend Joan Naylor sitting next to her. Families represented here are the Farrants, the Haywards, the Leonards, and the Cowleys. Also to be seen are May Bush, June Perrett, Pete Gunning, Margaret Smith, and Mrs Kelly, the choirmaster's wife.

Some of the congregation of the Tudor Road Methodist church pictured *c.* 1949, during Mr Gibby's term of office.

The first pantomime staged by the Tudor Players was *Cinderella* in 1946. Here the cast take their curtain call: among those pictured are Jean Uren, Roy Cowley, Don Philpott, Alfie Rooks, Jean Hill, Pat Baker, Margaret Jefferies, Margaret Smith, and Davey Baker.

Some notable actors in this Tudor Players' production of *Little Women* included Arthur Sibley and Robert Lang, supported here by Ann Solway, Joyce Bartlett, Gloria Gaydon, Don and Beryl Philpott, Jean Uren, and Roy Cowley.

Another production which starred the now famous Robert Lang was *The Wind of Heaven*. He stands in the doorway surveying the action, Jack Elve sits by the door, Gloria Gaydon reposes by the hearth, Jean Uren is dressed in cap and apron and Don Philpott stands behind the table; Joyce Bartlett looks on.

In the 1947 production of *Good Friday* Jack Boswell, the producer and driving force behind the Players, made this rare stage appearance as the blind beggar.

17

Roy Cowley, Don Philpott, Joyce Bartlett, Ann Solway, and Arthur Sibley made up the cast of *Granite*.

The *Ladies in Retirement* are Joyce Bartlett, Jean Uren, Beryl Philpott, Betty Jenkins, and June Perrett in 1949. In later years Jean, who specialized in regional accents, appeared in several radio productions.

Love blooms for two of the Players. Here Jean Uren and Roy Cowley are surrounded by their parents and best man Jack Boswell. The bridesmaids are Roy's sister, Janet (left), and Jean's sister, Joyce (right), and Doreen Sutton, who later married Brian Cowley, Roy's brother.

Down to Belle Vue Road, 1950s. This corner of High Street was later pulled down, together with all the other properties in the row, only to be replaced by two small litter-strewn parks. The only building still standing is the hardware shop, then Savory's and now owned by Mr Ahmed. Do you remember the police boxes like this one on the corner of Washington Avenue?

Garmston's cycle shop on the corner of Belle Vue Road and the lower part of Greenbank Avenue, 1920s. It was to become one of the casualties of the 1960s replanning.

A last glance at Belle Vue Road before we move on. Visible, far left in the background of this peaceful, car-free view from the early part of this century, are the buildings which were demolished in the 1970s in favour of a sheltered housing complex .

Belle Vue Road, Easton, Bristol 5.

Two
Eastville

This segment of the area was always regarded as being a bit upmarket, possessing, as it did, rather grander houses – one's prestige rose the closer one lived to Muller Road and Eastville Park. The bus depot was also situated here for the 2 and 2a routes (Lockleaze and Frenchay respectively). How our hearts would sink when the driver climbed out of his cab and he and the conductor walked off together into the depot! It could often mean quite a long wait. Indecision time then – should we sit it out or get out and walk? If we made up our minds to follow the latter course, it always seemed to be odds on that the bus would sail past us before we reached the Thirteen Arches!

The bottom of Robertson Road, showing Alice Howard's hairdressing salon, 1950s. Alice, herself, is seen here on the right, in the company of Mrs Purcell, the wife of a well-known local doctor. Next door can be glimpsed the newsagent's, conveniently close to the No. 83 bus stop. In the 1980s these two shops were adapted to form one store – a mini-market run by the Kalsi family. Later, it came under different ownership but, due to the competition of the new Tesco store built in Eastgate, the store closed and the property has been boarded up for the past few years.

Just down the road, by the traffic lights, stands an imposing building, seen here in the days when it was still the White Swan. Later it was used by Unigate Dairies as a social club and is now a bed and breakfast hostel.

2	H12085	LOCKLEAZE — EASTVILLE — OLD MARKET — LAWRENCE WESTON	2

ROUTE : Romney Avenue, Shaldon Road, Muller Road, Stapleton Road, Stapleton Road Station, Trinity Road, West Street, Old Market Street, Lower Castle Street, Penn Street, Bond Street, Marlborough Street, Upper Maudlin Street, Perry Road, Park Row, Queen's Road, Whiteladies Road, The Downs, Stoke Road, Druid Hill, Shirehampton Road, Kingsweston Road, Kingsweston Lane, Long Cross, Chapel Lane, Beverston Gardens.

MONDAYS TO FRIDAYS

	am	am	am	am	am		am	am	am	am		pm		pm	pm		pm	pm	pm	pm	pm
Lockleaze (Gainsboro' Sq.) ....dep.	5 34	......	......	......	6 7	Then every	8 43	8 52	9 4	9 13	Then	3 1	Then every	4 1	4 7	Then every	5 55	6 7	6 16	6 28	6 37
Eastville Junction .... ,,	5 45	5 54	6 0	6 6	6 18	12 mins. from	8 54	9 3	9 15	9 24	every	3 12	12 mins. from	4 12	4 18	12 mins. from	6 6	6 18	6 27	6 39	6 48
Old Market (Lwr. Castle Street) ... ,,	5 54	6 3	6 9	6 15	6 27	Lockleaze &	9 3	9 12	9 24	9 33	12	3 21	Lockleaze &	4 21	4 27	Lockleaze &	6 15	6 27	6 36	6 48	6 57
The Downs .... ,,	6 7	6 16	6 22	6 28	6 40	every 6 mins.	9 16	9 25	9 37	9 46	mins.	3 34	every 6 mins.	4 34	4 40	every 6 mins.	6 28	6 40	6 49	7 1	7 10
Sea Mills (Square) .... ,,	6 17	6 26	6 32	6 38	6 50	from Eastville	9 26	9 35	9 47	9 56	until	3 44	from Eastville	4 44	4 50	from Eastville	6 38	6 50	6 59	7 11	7 20
Lawrence Weston .... arr.	6 27	6 36	6 42	6 48	7 0	until	9 36	9 45	9 57	10 6		3 54	until	4 54	5 0	until	6 48	7 0	7 9	7 21	7 30

	pm		pm	pm	pm	pm	pm
Lockleaze (Gainsboro' Sq.) ....dep.	6 52	Then	1052	11 7	1115	1130	1145
Eastville Junction .... ,,	7 3	every	11 3	1118	1126	1141	1156
Old Market (Lr. Castle Street) ...... ,,	7 12	15	1112	1127	......	......	....
The Downs .... ,,	7 25	mins.	1125	1140	......	......	......
Sea Mills (Square) .... ,,	7 35	until	1135	1150	......	......	....
Lawrence Weston .... arr.	7 45		1145	12 0			

	am	am	am	am	am		am	am	
Lawrence Weston .... dep.	5 16	6 6	6 14	6 24	6 30	Then every	8 6	8 12	Then every
Sea Mills (Square) .... ,,	5 27	6 17	6 25	6 35	6 41	6 mins. to	8 17	8 23	6 mins. to
The Downs .... ,,	5 37	6 27	6 35	6 45	6 51	Eastville &	8 27	8 33	Eastville &
Old Market Street .... ,,	5 50	6 40	6 48	6 58	7 4	every 12 mins.	8 40	8 46	every 12 mins.
Eastville Junction .... ,,	5 59	6 49	6 57	7 7	7 13	to Lockleaze	8 49	8 55	to Lockleaze
Lockleaze (Gainsboro' Sq.) arr.	6 11	7 1	......	......	7 25	until	9 1	9 7	until

	am	am		pm	pm		pm	pm		pm	pm	pm	pm	pm	pm	pm	pm	pm	pm		pm	pm	pm	pm
Lawrence Weston ....dep.	9 12	9 21	Then	3 21	3 30	Then every	5 30	5 33	.....	5 39	5 45	5 51	5 57	6 3	6 9	6 15	6 21	6 27	6 33	Then	1033	1048	11 3	1118
Sea Mills (Square) .... ,,	9 23	9 32	every	3 32	3 41	6 mins. to	5 41	5 44	.....	5 50	5 56	6 2	6 8	6 14	6 20	6 26	6 32	6 38	6 44	every	1044	1059	1114	1129
The Downs .... ,,	9 33	9 42	12	3 42	3 51	Eastville &	5 51	5 54	.....	6 0	6 6	6 12	6 18	6 24	6 30	6 36	6 42	6 48	6 54	15	1054	11 9	1124	1139
Old Market Street .... ,,	9 46	9 55	mins.	3 55	4 4	every 12 mins.	6 4	6 7	......	6 13	6 19	6 25	6 31	6 37	6 43	6 49	6 55	7 1	7 7	mins.	11 7	1122	1137	1152
Eastville Junction .... ,,	9 55	10 4	until	4 4	4 13	to Lockleaze	6 13	6 16	.....	6 22	6 28	6 34	6 40	6 46	6 52	6 58	7 4	7 10	7 16	until	1116	1131	1146	12 1
Lockleaze (Gainsboro' Sq.) ...... arr.	10 7	1016		4 16	4 25	until	6 25	...	.....	6 34	6 40	..	6 52	...	7 4	......	7 16	.....	7 28		1128	1143	.....	......

SATURDAYS

	am	am	am		am	am	am	am	am		pm	pm	pm	pm	pm	pm	pm	pm	pm	pm	pm	pm	pm	
Lockleaze (Gainsboro' Sq.) ....dep.	5 34	......	6 1	Then	1013	..	1025	1031	.....	Then every	.....	4 55	5 4	5 16	5 25	5 37	5 49	6 1	6 13	6 25	6 37	6 42	6 52	Then
Eastville Junction .... ,,	5 45	6 0	6 12	every	1024	1030	1036	1042	1048	12 mins. from	5 0	5 6	5 15	5 27	5 36	5 48	6 0	6 12	6 24	6 36	6 48	6 53	7 3	as
Old Market (Lwr. Castle Street) ... ,,	5 54	6 9	6 21	12	1033	1039	1045	1051	1057	Lockleaze &	5 9	5 15	5 24	5 36	5 45	5 57	6 9	6 21	6 33	6 45	6 57	....	7 12	Mondays
The Downs .... ,,	6 7	6 22	6 34	mins.	1046	1052	1058	11 4	1110	every 6 mins.	5 22	5 28	5 37	5 49	5 58	6 10	6 22	6 34	6 46	6 58	7 10	.....	7 25	to
Sea Mills (Square) .... ,,	6 17	6 32	6 44	until	1056	11 2	11 8	1114	1120	from Eastville	5 32	5 38	5 47	5 59	6 8	6 20	6 32	6 44	6 56	7 8	7 20	......	7 35	Fridays
Lawrence Weston .... arr.	6 27	6 42	6 54		11 6	1112	1118	1124	1130	until	5 42	5 48	5 57	6 9	6 18	6 30	6 42	6 54	7 6	7 18	7 30	......	7 45	

	am	am	am	am		am	am		pm	pm	pm	pm	pm	pm	pm		pm	pm	pm	pm	pm	
Lawrence Weston ....dep.	5 16	6 3	6 12	6 21	Then	1045	1054	Then every	4 18	4 24	4 30	4 36	4 42	4 48	4 57	Then every	5 45	5 54	6 6	6 21	6 33	Then
Sea Mills (Square) .... ,,	5 27	6 14	6 23	6 32	every	1056	11 5	6 mins. to	4 29	4 35	4 41	4 47	4 53	4 59	5 8	6 mins. to	5 56	6 5	6 17	6 32	6 44	as
The Downs .... ,,	5 37	6 24	6 33	6 42	12	11 6	1115	Eastville &	4 39	4 45	4 51	4 57	5 3	5 9	5 18	Eastville &	6 6	6 15	6 27	6 42	6 54	Mondays
Old Market Street .... ,,	5 50	6 37	6 46	6 55	mins	1119	1128	every 12 mins.	4 52	4 58	5 4	5 10	5 16	5 22	5 31	every 12 mins.	6 19	6 28	6 40	6 55	7 7	to
Eastville Junction .... ,,	5 59	6 46	6 55	7 4	until	1128	1137	to Lockleaze	5 1	5 7	5 13	5 19	5 25	5 31	5 40	to Lockleaze	6 28	6 37	6 49	7 4	7 16	Fridays
Lockleaze (Gainsboro' Sq.) .... arr.	6 11	6 58	7 7	7 16		1140	1149	until	5 13	5 19	......	5 31	......	5 43	5 52	until	6 40	6 49	7 1	7 16	7 28	

ADDITIONAL JOURNEYS : Mondays to Fridays, Eastville to Lockleaze 5-20 a.m., 5-53, 6-17, 6-29, 6-41, 7-1 a.m.
Saturdays ,, ,, ,, 5-20 a.m., 5-47, 6-11, 6-23, 6-35 a.m.

Bus timetable from 1959.

Eastville Primitive Methodist church in 1971. The destruction of what we locals called 'Lower Stapleton Road' or simply 'The Lower Road' had already begun in order to make way for the M32. A complete rank of shops on the left-hand side was demolished: a confectioner's, a fish and chip shop, an off-licence, a hardware store, a grocery business and some very large stone houses. The church lingered on for a short while longer.

The Easton Primitive Methodist church choir in the late 1940s. A stark office block now stands on the site of the church. From left to right, back row: Cyril Fursman (organist), George Young. Third row: Fred Harris, Mr Dark, Reg Ware, Len Lindsay, Fred Lindsay, Jim Saunders, Bill Hill, Mr Ware. Second row: Graham Lindsay, Rita Willies, Anita Sanders (née Lewis), Mr Lewis, Elsie Lindsay, Margaret Tovey, Phyllis Dyer, Frances Ware. Front row: Mavis Dyer, Maureen Wadey (née Matthews), Frances Bromham (née Barnes), Freda Iles, Ellen Hill, Doris Holland, Ivy Parsons, Margaret Ware.

Smele's fish and greengrocery shop from the days when Eastville was packed with all sorts of trades: an opticians, a gents' outfitters, Hince's drapery store, J.H. Mills the grocers, Olivers Shoes, two wine shops, a post office, a butchery, two bakers, an ironmonger's, a dress shop, and a flower shop. The only retail businesses now are Mary Oliphant, chemist, the chicken take-away and the Monte Carlo café.

Two views of the Black Swan provided by Mike Tozer, the first around the turn of the century, the second in the 1930s. Isn't that lamppost glorious?

Opposite: The floods of 1968 – at least these three lads seem to be enjoying themselves! In the background can be seen the long-established butcher's presided over by the debonair Les Sheppard, one of a prominent family pursuing this trade in the city. His delivery lad, Sid Purnell, took over another of his shops further down Stapleton Road in the 1960s and now runs a thriving business on the corner of Clark Street. On the side wall of C.E. Brown's can be seen an advertisement dating from the time when the shop was owned by J.H. Mills, the forerunner of the Gateway chain. Edyth's flower shop, a little architectural gem, suffered severe structural damage in this flood and had to be demolished a few years later. This area is now the Black Swan car park.

Although Lloyds Bank still occupies the same site, everything else has changed since this picture was take in the early years of the century. The façade of the bank, too, has been altered to a more modern design.

A sunny afternoon in Stapleton Road, c. 1920. Colston's undertakers survives to the present day, although the business is now run by the Cotton brothers. In the distance can be seen the old workhouse – No. 100 Fishponds Road. The horse manure in the road would, I suspect, have been swiftly collected by keen rose-growers.

A tranquil Eastville scene showing His Majesty's Picture Palace in all its former glory. It was later renamed the Concorde and closed down in the 1980s.

A closer look at our premier local cinema. The shops beyond are all now used as cash and carry warehouses and the large building on the left has long since lost its façade, thus enabling the pavement to be widened considerably.

The same section of Stapleton Road viewed from the other direction near to where Tudball's the tailors and its affiliated drapery shop stood. All the shops have lost their upper bays in the intervening years with the last retail business closing in the 1980s.

A little further down the road in the direction of the station we come upon the Railway Inn, squashed in between Mann's the newsagent and a large brick warehouse. It is now vastly altered and renamed the Coach House. The newsagents and Ball's the fruiterers next door are long gone and HSS Hire covers the space where the warehouse stood.

Let us backtrack now and wander down some little streets which vanished at the same time as the 'Lower Road' – down Redding Road, now just a pathway leading to the Stadium (another casualty). We turn down Wolseley Road into Napier Road, a truncated portion of which still remains. Here we come upon two families carrying on old traditions. At the intersection of these streets stood the Crowcombe Forge. This picture shows Mr R. Crowcombe in the 1930s as photographed by Mr Sissons, the Eastville optician, whose shop was next door to Dr Purcell's surgery.

The refurbished premises run by Mr Crowcombe's son are shown here prior to the demolition of the buildings.

500-YEAR-OLD CRAFT IS
DOING NICELY, THANKS

At No. 69 Napier Road time seemed to stand still. The original caption for this newspaper photograph read: 'For at least 500 years the Osborn family have made whip thongs, and this picture shows two of the present members of the family plaiting the hide in the workshop in Eastville by the same method as that used by their forefathers.'

...istol
...mily
...adition

500-Years-Old
...ft Still Followed

... long lash of an expertly ...d stock-whip snakes above ...ssing heads of a herd of ... on the plains of Canada. ...ys are rounding up the ...

...ord Mayor of Bristol is riding ... His coachman carries a whip ...ong handle of holly or yew and ...w lash that is more ceremonial ...ful.

... of these scenes is linked to ...by one fact. The whip thongs ...de by an Eastville family who ...bably the only remaining crafts-... their kind in the West.

...rnest Osborn works alone at his ...h Bellevue-road. In a workshop ...er-road his three brothers and a ... can be seen any day cutting ... of hide and plaiting them into ...that will go all over the country ...ps the world.

...t least 500 years the Osborn ... have made whip-thongs that ...rected the carriages of nobility ...yalty, been used by members of ...int in the country, as well as for ...oaches, four-in-hands, brakes, ... and drays.

CORNISH ORIGIN

...ead of the family lived in Corn-... the fifteenth century, and at the ...the nineteenth the grandfather ...eneration which represents the ...day came to Bristol to found a ... here.

...ourse we have had our ups and ... Mr. Ernest Osborn told me, ...n "Evening World" reporter. ...the motor-car drove the horse ... road we wondered what we ...do, and were forced to turn our ...n to dog leads and collars and ...

...in the last few years there has ...

This Family's Speciality is Whip Thongs

IN the Eastville district of Bristol four brothers and a nephew are keeping alive a centuries-old family tradition.

For at least 500 years the Osborn family has been plaiting whip thongs. The craft, it is definitely known, has been handed down from father to son since the 15th century—when an ancestor carried on the trade in Cornwall. Probably earlier Osborns plaited their thongs.

Exactly the same methods as they employed are used to-day. There is no machinery—nothing but a sharp knife, a thumbnail for a gauge, and a great deal of skill to slice the expensive cow, goat and kangaroo hides with a minimum of wastage.

Thongs made by Mr. Ernest Osborn, his three brothers and nephew, are used all over the country and in many parts of the world by hunting folk, dog breeders and ranchers. Osborn thongs have directed the carriages of royalty for generations. They were used in the Jubilee procession and will probably play their little part in the Coronation.

Several stunt stockwhip-wielders of the stage have had giant thongs specially made in the Osborn workshops. Mr. Ernest Osborn's record is one 24 ft. long.

"There are not many plaiters left, and I believe we are the last in the West Country," Mr. Ernest Osborn told the *Sunday Pictorial.* "We suffered, of course, when horses nearly disappeared from the roads, but now the luxury side of the trade is flourishing. New riding schools are springing up, and we have to work hard to keep pace with the demand."

MATCH-MAKER MAYOR

The Mayor of Bridgwater, Mr. F. J. Reed, will have the pleasure of attending a wedding which he arranged between strangers.

A few weeks ago a Cardiff widower with four children wrote a letter begging the Mayor to help him to find a bride. The Mayor's appeal produced 100 replies from women ranging from domestic servants to private secretaries, and from nearly every county between Lancashire and Cornwall.

The widower has chosen a West Country woman as his bride. They met at Mr. Reed's home, are now engaged, and wedding bells will ring in Christmas.

Model village with working figures driven by wind-power has been erected by Mr. Harold S. Ham, of Elm Tree Farm, Ware, near Axbridge, Somerset.

Air Minist...
Propose...
Centre fo...

...Welsh authorit... ...tion and Penybont R... asked by the Air Minist... on a proposal to esta... extending from Sker... the shores of the Brist...

The Penybont Coun... with the residents who... reply to the Ministry... information has been c... Members of the Cou... day were favourably d...

Other works to b... locality by the Gover... factory at Bridgen... from the proposed h... aerodrome at St. At... from Bridgend, for... The construction of t... by the inhabitants. Th... cil yesterday forwarded... Office assuring wholeh... the erection of the fact...

British Le...
Did N...

The biggest accompli... Legion in the West Co... to-day when the Field o... cated at St. Gregory's C... R.A.F. planes will be... when the shrine is unv... will be broadcast to hu... a field overlooking the... The Exeton and Distri... are responsible for the... F. W. C Featherstone-... man of the British Le... unveiling ceremony. T... Very Reverend Harry F... duct the service.

30

286 & 288 Hodders Ltd. chemists
286A, Hoare Geo. Hy
——Warwick Road & Warwick Avenue intersect
318 Pratt & Faull, physcns. & surgns
318 Faull Jn. Langdon M.R.C.S., L.R.C.P.Lond., D.P.M.Lond. physician & surgn
318 Pratt Gordon Wm. Fairtlough M.D., Ch.B.Dub. physcn. & surgn
322 Gillard Miss Mary Eliz
324 Kidd Hubert Lancey
326 Painter Miss May
328 Pitt Mervyn Fras
330 Heyward Arth. Chas
332 Horrell Mrs
334 Taylor Victor
336 Lawrence Edwd
338 & 340 Wyatt Wm. Jas. & Son, cycle dlr
342 & 344 Fox Edwd. Chas. leather mer
346 Daniell & Co. (H. H. Kidner, propr.), tobccnsts
348 Veal Jn. hairdrssr
350 & 352 Swain's Temperance Hotel
——Fox Road intersects
354 West Victor, fishmngr
356 Haskins Geo. Wm. baker
358 Mutter Miss Harriett, confctnr
360 Pickett Arth. Edwd
362 Witchell Miss Doris, tripe dlr
366 Ashman Chas. J. furniture remover
370 Edwards Francis & Son, florist
372 Hales Gilbt. Jas. boot repr
374 Webb Harold Geo. dining rms
376 Ball Hy. Geo greengro
378 Mann Arth. Hy. Burrow, newsagt
380 Railway Inn (Fredk. Ruddock)
——Robert Street intersects
388 Gibbs Kenneth Donald, cycle dlr
390 Milton J. S. Ltd. bakers
392 Glenside Furnishers (P. T. Banning, propr)
394 Pole Harold, butcher
396 Wood Philip H. undertaker
398 Pearce Geo. Edwd. Chas. amusement arcade
400 Sylvia, ladies' hairdrssrs
402 Force Wm. outfitter
404 Paintmore Co. paint mers
406 Wadsworth Wltr. refrshmnt. rms
408 Strode Cosh & Penfold Ltd. chemists
410 Woodward Wltr. Jn. butcher
412 Spear E. W. piano depot
414 Pearks Dairies Limited
416 Mitchell E.A.Ltd. wine & spirit mers
418 Burnard A. & Co. tailors
420 & 422 Mapstone Mrs. J. tobccnst
424 His Majesty's (The Eastville Hippodrome Co. Ltd)
Bristol Sanitary Authority Dust Destructor
Ross L. A. (engnr.'s residence)
Bristol Rovers Football Club Ltd.—Charles F. Ferrari, sec. (office, Eastville stadium)
Eastville Supporters' Club—R. B. Marsh, hon. sec. (Eastville stadium)
Bristol Greyhound Racing Association Ltd. (Eastville stadium)
Eastville Greyhound Racing Club—Chas. F. Ferrari, sec
438 Black Swan Hotel (Wltr. E. Pollard)
438 National Society of Painters
Monarch Coaches (Bristol) Ltd. motor coach proprs
438 Prosser A. G. motor engnr
440 Coneybeer Mrs. Edith, florist
440A, Cottle F. C. & Son, cabnt. mkrs
442 Mills J. H. Ltd. grocers
444 Sheppard C. butcher
446 Lewton Alfd. F. wine & spirit retlr
448 Burridge's Bakeries (Bristol) Ltd
450 Palmer & Ashford, statnrs
Post & M. O. Office
——Redding Road intersects
452 Bollom of Bristol Ltd. dyers & cleaners
454 Hardwell Regnld. Geo. butcher
456 Stone F. W. (S. L. Phelps, propr.), ironmngr
458 Lewis's Stores, grocers
460 Rodbourn Miss Maud, furniture dlr
462 Wood Lenric
464 Reynalds & Purcell, physcns. & surgns
464 Purcell Jn. M.B., B.Ch., B.A.O. physcn. & surgn
468 Sisson R. P. Ltd. F.B.O.A. opticians
470 Brooks Rd. Alfd. newsagt
472 Prosser Mrs. Mary Olive, wool stores
474 Brown Wm. Fredk
476 Marshall Ernest Edwd
478 Honkins Hopkin Edwd
480 Phibben Ernest Hy
482 Sharp Thos. A
484 Lovell Jn. Edwd
486 Williams Edwd

488 Tulk Miss Ivy Beatrice, shopkpr
490 Long Wm. Chas. dairyman
492 Taylor Miss Ada Ann
492 Cook Mrs. S. J
494 Harris Ernest
496 Williams Wm. Sydney
498 Public Window Cleaning & Carpet Beating Co.—Gilbt. Watts, propr
500 Prosser Jn. Hy
502 Wookey Albt. Jas. & Son, plumbers
——Napier Road intersects
504 Mayne Mrs. Lily Rosina
506 Champeny Mrs. Alice
508 Griffiths Hy. Chas
510 Hodge Mrs. Florence E
512 Scull Ernest Hy
512 Lacey Kenneth
514 Hill Ronald Arth
516 Godfrey Eric Wm. H
518 Larcombe Miss Lucy M. costumier
520 Brookman Fredk
522 Dyment Miss Ethel
524 Moody Leslie Jeffrey, confctnr
526 Jenkins Mrs. Florence, beer retlr
528 Coles Mrs. Rosina, shopkpr
530 Whiting Edwd. oil & colour stores
532 Fox Alfd
534 Carpenter Jn. Edwd
536 Matthews Mrs. Rose Ann
538 Gunter Wm. fried fish dlr
540 Wakeham Jn. Lyndall
542 Alway Mrs. Annie
544 Fox Edwd
546 Lamborn Mrs. Eliz. shopkpr
546 Lamborn Thos. Jas
550 Hanbry Regnld
552 Phillips Arth
554 Chard Mrs. Eliz. grocer
556 Green Alfd
558 Berry Capt. Harry N.model ship mkr
560 Sleigh Mrs. Kate
560 Collins Arth
562 Nethercott Wm
564 Merchant Albt. Edwin
566 Sugg Mrs. Florence Mabel
568 Cox Albt
570 Harris Geo. Edwd
572 Watts Albt. Hy
574 Parsloe Mrs. Emily
576 Williams Wm. Hy
Harris Norman Collingwood (Viaduct Filling Station)
590 Harris Norman Collingwood, refrshmnt. rms
592 Jenkins Alfd
594 Griffee F. E. Ltd. bldrs
——Railway Viaduct crosses here
606 Hall Jn. Hy
608 King Ernest Chas
610 Williams Alfd. Lewis
612 Jarrett Jas. Albt
614 Linton Jas. newsagt
616 Davey Thos. Jas. grocer
——Muller Road intersects
618 Wilson Mrs. Hilda
620 McGrath Lawrence
622 Poole Jn. Wm
624 Allpass Herbt. Geo
626 Hawkins Ronald Geo
626 Beak Wltr. Jas
628 Lewis Howard Llewellyn
630 Matthews Gilbt. Hy
632 McGovern Mrs. Ada
634 Stevens Archbld
636 Baker Stephen Hy
638 Weeks Mrs. Rosina
640 Blackmore Saml
642 Clode Fras. Hy
644 Price Ivor
646 Brown Ernest Jn
648 Hares Arth
650 Blake Wm. Fras
652 Baxter Mrs. Ethel May
654 Hewlett Arth. Jas
656 Higgs Miss Mabel Amy Edith
656 Stone Fredk. Gordon
658 Dicker Jas. Rd
660 Banks Miss Clara Kathln. S.R.N., S.C.M. municipal midwife
660 Stuart Miss Sarah Eliz. B.A., S.R.N., S.C.M. municipal midwife
662 Hollyman Mrs. Florence
664 Harris Harry
666 Hepburn Edgar
668 Cox Stanley Geo
670 Phillips Miss Caroline
672 Hobbs Mrs. Lillie
674 Mason Mrs. Mary
676 Williams Miss Doris
678 Hares Wm
680 Paske Fredk
682 Bull Fredk. Jas
684 Krichell Thos
686 Carr Regnld
688 Pummell Ernest Wltr
690 Stone Wm
692 Jones Herbt. Wm
694 Williams Hy. Edwd
696 Spragg Albt. Edwd

STAPLETON ROAD—continued.
698 Haines Jsph. Thos
700 Boalch Arth. Edwd
702 Attwood Frank Stanley
704 Greedy Wm. Hy
706 Wallace Jn. Nelson
708 Boyce Wm. Jas
710 Swanson Ernest Victor
712 Hitchcock Wm. Tom
714 Willis Hy. Jas
716 Lusty Frank Aug
716 Lusty F. A. Ltd. builders
——Cottrell Road intersects
718 Court Wm
here cross over
Merchants Arms (Mrs. Ada Viole Williams)
EASTVILLE PARK
——Muller Road intersects
——Railway Viaduct crosses here
597 Chilcott Harold, nurseryman
597 Sillitoe Ralph
——Freemantle Road intersects
595 Gane & Quick, upholsterers
595 Robinson Evan Owen
593 Ridler Edwin
591 Taylor Miss Rose Emma
589 Witts G. A. & Sons Ltd. pastry cooks
——Sandy Lane intersects
583 Hooper Edwd. Wltr
581 Upton Ernest Philip
579 Brackley Albt. Fredk
577 Taylor Saml. Hy
575 Bisp Harold Edwd
573 Williams Hy. Jas
571 Williams Ernest, piano tuner
——Heath Street intersects
569 Harris Mrs. Mary Ann, beer retlr
567 Paull Chas. greengro
565 Bishop Geo. Hy
563 Stevens Fredk
561 Bird Vivian Alfd
559 Bidder Peter Chas
557 Luff Mrs. Mary Sarah
555 Boddie Mrs. Sarah Jane
553 Lane Fredk. Chas
——Glen Park intersects
551 Marsh Rupert Chas
549 Woodman Miss
547 Maxted Mrs. Matilda
545 Porter Regnld. Thos. decrtr
525 Porter Jr.
543 Sloman Thos. Jn
543 Wilcox Kenneth Geo
541 Whiting Wm
539 Lea-Jones Nigel Arth. wardrobe dlr
——Boswell Street intersects
537 Woods Fras. Hy. Geo. shopkpr
535 Willies Wm. house furnisher
533 Phyllis (Harry Notton), ladie hairdrssr
523 Scoggins Saml. Arth
521 Williams Mrs. Caroline
519 Palmer Thos
517 Bessell Edmnd. Geo
515 Tanner Fredk. Arth
513 Roberts Jn
511 Moody Edwd. Jas
509 Clarke Mrs. Clara
507 Dunsford Wltr. Jn
505 Ellis Arth. Ernest
——Argyle Street intersects
503 March Wm. Hy.
503 Ashton Jn
501 Lloyd Wm
499 Hooker Alfd. Jas
497 Harris.Edwd
495 Edwards Regnld. Frank
493 Harris Mrs. Ethel
491 Sanbells Edwd
489 Newport Mrs. Annie Barlow
487 Dodd Mrs
485 Hayward Mrs
483 Sheppard Mrs. Charlotte
483 Webb Chas
481 Bennett Fredk. Ethering
METHODIST CHURCH
——here are Fishponds Road Robertson Road
443 Westminster Bank Ltd. (Eastvil branch)—Percy Jn. Arth. Bank manager
443 Evans Chas. E
441 Moxham Percy Gilbt. hosier
439 Blake A. E. & G. boot mkrs
437 Stokes C. A. chemist & druggist
435 National Provincial Bank Lt (Eastville branch)—S. M. Burki manager
435 Fry Edwd. caretaker
433 Hill Thos. Jas. fruitr
431 Colston Edwd. undertaker
425, 427 & 429 Hince Ernest E. (Connet Ltd.), drapers
425 Bailey Wilfred Ernest
425 Bailey W. E. & E. J. Osborne, tu commssn. agts

Now we've come so far we simply must hurry along the Lower Road, past Wookey's the plumbers and Whiting's the ironmongers (related to the Naylors who ran a similar business in St Mark's Road) and all the other well-remembered little shops to view, once again, the Thirteen Arches, that impressive landmark close by the Muller Road traffic lights, providing a backcloth here to a 1930s ice-cream vendor.

The famous Thirteen Arches as seen from one of the entrances to the Rovers' ground. Many people gathered there on that chilly, misty day in 1968 to watch the destruction of this great monument to railway engineering. How graceful the structure was compared to the ugly concrete motorway which now dominates the vista.

The first explosives failed to shift the stalwart bridge. It seem determined to defy attempts to destroy it.

Two aerial views (courtesy of Ben Bird) showing the area being prepared for the construction of the M32 and the Eastgate shopping centre.

Three
St Mark's Church and Environs

It is hard to imagine the church without its sheltering cloak of tightly packed little streets, yet little more than a hundred years ago all that existed was a handful of cottages in, and bordering, the grounds of the old manor house. In fact, my own house in St Mark's Road was originally a farm building with bits tacked on over the years. What is now my entrance hall was once the front garden with the front door facing towards the church. The building of the railway line in the 1840s opened up the area and when the coal mines became operational urban development accelerated with astonishing rapidity.

We will approach St Mark's Road via Mivart Street where we stop to admire the bunting and jostle through the crowd enjoying their VE Day party in 1945.

The name of Ashman used to be synonymous with St Mark's Road and it was a sad day when their business moved to Fishponds and the grand old house behind the shop was pulled down. Here is one of Charlie Ashman's original vehicles restored to sparkling splendour.

Outside the first shop owned by the Mahoti family, Ugandan refugees forced to flee from Idi Amin's regime, St Mark's Road, 1970s. Over the years the family has built up a successful business and the shop has been extended through the acquisition of adjacent properties. No. 80 was formerly run by Lily Best as a draper's shop: there everything could seemingly be purchased, from a lace collar to a baby's rompers.

A desolate view of Nos 77, 79, and 81, St Mark's Road. The first two shops were once the fondly remembered Daily Want hardware shop while, at No. 81, Mount-stevens opened their first bakery. Not long after this photograph was taken in the late 1980s, Satwinder Bhogal took over No. 79, later extending his pharmacy to take in No. 81. No. 77 has also been renovated and serves as an office dealing with racial issues.

Local people say a fond farewell to Mrs Edwards, a popular post-lady, 1970s. There have been many changes made to the background shops since that time. In 1973 they included: Lewis's (grocers), Herbert Edbrooke (butcher), Ali Mohammed (general store), Geoff Snell (newsagent), Mrs Perry (greengrocer), G.R. Clothing Co., Roberts (baker), Parfrey's (electrical equipment), and Flair (hairdressers). On the corner of Henrietta Street was Sta-Tex dry cleaners.

Extracts from the log book of St Mark's National School

1874

Three lads sentenced to a week's imprisonment for stealing fruit.

A. Johnstone threw a stick at Elizabeth Cox wounding her face, and he kicked her hat about the room, all in the presence of the pupil-teacher (*) who was blamed for not preventing the occurrence. [* At this time schools advertised for paupers to become pupil-teachers.]

Five or six boys threw mud through the window at the girls who stayed back to dinner.

1875

96 boys and 60 girls.

24 May

One child died (smallpox), and Louisa Brown of low fever. Children sent home for school fees and parents now to write notes if a child has been absent.

6 June

Frank King (little boy) accidentally killed on a timber wagon. Edward Brown has died.

Sept.

Boys and girls separated. 116 boys, 67 girls.

1876

Formal opening of Girls School. New room will not begin as a girls' school until May.

Several children expelled for gross irregularity.

March

Several of irregular children's parents summoned and fined by the St George School Board. One of the parents came to the school and made a great disturbance. Had to send for a policeman before she would go away.

102 boys and 55 girls.

School Attendance Officer has too wide a district to make children regular.

July

School treat to Ridgway Lawn. 430 day and Sunday school scholars. [A holiday was given when the schoolroom was wanted for a tea meeting, missionary meeting, or bazaar; also, when there was only one teacher to cope owing to illness and there was no-one to teach the boys.]

1877

Jan.

Singing and drawing classes commence. Fee 1d per week.

12 March

Log book torn by some malicious person. It has been locked up in my drawer and therefore someone must have a key. Money missed from the missionary boxes and lock wrenched off cupboard.

March

Edwin Jones, the pupil-teacher, told a great number of lies. He had given notice that he was going as a military cadet to Woolwich by the aid of his uncle, a retired officer, and asked to go immediately as his orders had come through. Committee contacted his father and found the lad had enlisted in the 10th Hussars and was to start at Canterbury the next day. Vicar wrote to the War Office concerning the affair. No assistance for many weeks.

7–11 May

Parents complain that their children are taught by boys as small as themselves. We are trying to get a lad from St Simon's named E. Fitzpatrick as a monitor. He is only 12 but in size seems to be 17 or 18.

11–15 June

The large board school in Frogmarsh is being rapidly completed. I expect many of our children will be drawn off.

Collecting funds for the tea party at Ridgway Lawn. Hired the Union Band to go.

Very successful outing.

Reaching the church we must pause for a word with Revd Walter Booker, a well-loved vicar. A shy man, he lived alone in the vast vicarage although he did employ a housekeeper whose task it was to walk his large boisterous dog. The poor lady used to be dragged down St Mark's Road at about 50mph!

Were these ladies preparing for some sort of function at the church? My grandmother is second from right and the vicar is Revd Robinson, or could it be Mr Penfold, the curate who baptized me in 1940?

The St Mark's Church Guide Troop in the late 1920s. May Evans is among them in the middle of the back row.

May 25 (Sun.)—**Whitsunday.** Holy Communion at 7, 8, and 9.30 a.m.
  ,, 26 (Mon.)—**Monday in Whitsun Week.** Holy Communion at 7.30 a.m.
  ,, 27 (Tues.)—**Tuesday in Whitsun Week.** Holy Communion at 8 a.m.
  ,, 28 (Wed.)—Holy Communion at 9.30 a.m. Mothers' Union Meeting at 3 p.m. Speaker, Mrs. Havard-Perkins.
  ,, 29 (Thurs.)—Holy Communion at 7 a.m.

PARISH REGISTERS.

Holy Baptism.

Mar. 23—Nicholas William George Sowden.
  ,, 23—Peter Leonard Brinton.
  ,, 23—Michael Joyce.
  ,, 30—Dorothy Lilly Bellamy.
  ,, 30—David Stephen Bellamy.
April 6—Stephen Charles Pearce.
  ,,   6—Rodney William Cox.
  ,,   6—Beverley Reginald Morgan.
  ,, 12—Roger Nigel John Fellender.
  ,, 13—Diane Geraldine Hughes.
  ,, 13—Janet Ann Gibney.
  ,, 13—Rex James Rimell.

Confirmation.

The following were Confirmed by the Bishop of Malmesbury, at St. Agnes Church, on Friday, March 14th :—
    Victor Colin Taylor and David Ernest Vale.
    Lillie Rose Osborne (Mrs.) and Phyllis Edna May Price (Miss).
    We welcome them into the **full** Communicant fellowship of the Church.

Holy Matrimony.

Mar. 29—Clifford Sidney Webber and Edna Florence Collins.
  ,, 31—Roy Shorney and Jean Miller.
April 5—Arthur Dennis Britton and Ivy Joyce Bessell.
  ,,   5—James Ypres Fisher and Nancy Margaret Thomas.
  ,,   5—Walter Greenwood Cave and Jean Gosling.
  ,,   5—Arthur Henry Broad and Winifred May Morse.
  ,,   5—John Henry Grainger and Gwendoline Florence Spencer.
  ,,   7—Arthur John Love and Henrietta Hares.

Burial

Mar. 27—Peter Claire St. George, aged 15 months.
April 16—Alice Yorke, aged 82 years.

A page from the St Mark's, Easton parish magazine, May 1947.

Extract from the log book of St Mark's National School (Boys)

This was once sited in what is now the mosque and prior to that was St Mark's Church Hall.

1907

11 Jan: Attendance only 92 per cent. Much sickness.

23 Jan: Very cold morning, Temperature 40° at 10am.

14 Feb: Mr P. Rea inspected physical drill. Excellent.

16 May: Empire Day celebrations. Talks by managers and songs. *Flag of Britain* and Kipling's *Processional* were sung. Closed with cheers for the King, the Flag, and the visitors.

6 Jul: Photographs taken.

22 Jul: George James Skinner won Christchurch (?) scholarship tenable for 4 years and the value of £49.

23 Jul: Letter of complaint to parents of Vernon Baker respecting the very untidy state of his face, neck, etc.

24 Jul: Mr Baker (father) called at schoolroom indignant of the step taken concerning his son's state. Upon the class teacher substantiating my remarks, Mr Baker seemed to recognize that there had been legitimate cause for complaint from teachers.

6 Sept: 33 boys to zoo.

Mr Wait. 'The wasp'. Each boy through the microscope viewed the sting with poison bladder and the wonderful eye.

23 Oct: Desk found broken and many things disturbed by those attending a meeting last evening.

29 Oct: 13 boys to Dundry and Barrow reservoirs.

Lesson on specific properties of matter.

24 boys to Frome Valley.

1908

13 Feb: Coal not delivered (ordered on 3rd).

18 Feb: Two lads from Easton Council School discovered in the porch during the luncheon hour in the act of taking overcoats. Their headmaster contacted.

28 Feb: Mr Hicks after 10 years as Assistant Master resigned to become Assistant Master at St George Boys (near his home).

1 May: Mr Hicks asked for transfer back to St Mark's.

11 May: The curtain rod ordered to be placed between the two lower classes working in the main room has just been completed. The contractor has had it in hand 14 months!

19 May: A Mrs Tyndall who accompanied Mrs Pavey called this day and expressed regret at the part she had taken in supporting Mrs Pavey's complaint. She states that she has since found out that the lady obtained her support by deceit, in hiding from her the true facts of the case. Mrs Pavey had come to the school after receiving a note regarding her son's untidiness. She was very abusive but the headmaster took care to place the facts of the case.)

25 May: After the Empire Day Service Holiday the majority of the boys adjourned to the park to enjoy a game of cricket.

19 June: Formed a branch of the RED Brotherhood. This society encourages boys not to smoke until aged 16–20.

8 July: Special songs rehearsed for the 'Reception of the King' in tomorrow's procession and a few brief remarks made on the life of the King and Queen.

Our route now takes us along Albion Road and under the archway to another VE Day party for the people of Bannerman Road.

We have arrived now at Bannerman Road School, or Easton Board School as it was known until the 1930s. I had the privilege of escorting a group of ex-pupils around their old classrooms in the spring of 1997 and they were intrigued to examine their school records in the original log books. The future of the school is uncertain at present as it is in a bad state of repair. That aside, we had a wonderful day answering the questions of present-day scholars. 'Did you use quill pens?' one youthful-looking senior citizen was asked! In this picture Easton Board School pupils of the 1920s pose for the camera.

Easton Board School pupils of the 1930s.

Roy Cowley and classmates, c. 1936. Roy is third from the right at the front.

Roy's brother Les figures in this group. He is in the third row, third from the right.

Les Cowley is again among those pictured, second from the left, second row.

Junior boys class at Easton Board School, 1930s.

This picture of Easton Board School pupils is thought to date from 1936. Ivor Blake is in the front row, second from right. Gordon Hazell is on the far left of the front row, many years before he found fame.

On to the 1970s now and a more informal pose. My daughter, Amanda Britton, is in the centre in the pale jumper, looking as if she is about to cause a bit of disruption!

The Elmgrove Dairy used to trade just up All Hallows Road, to the back of the school. A rather frail-looking milkman makes deliveries in this lovely picture from the Mike Tozer collection.

Time to cross the road and push open the heavy door to All Hallows' Church Hall, venue of many Daisy Luxton dancing displays. Here, in 1946, the Cubs are preparing to be photographed, among them Maurice Fellows and Brian Wright (both to the left), Derek Marsh (the tall one), John Cross, Patrick Frape, Colin Downs, John Catley, Don Box, Brian Clayfield, Denis Justin (middle row), and Ken Greville, -?-, Bobby Jones, and David Norton (all in the front).

From the vicarage garden across the road, sweet music wafts on the summer air. It is June 1907 and, judging by the programme, we are in for a special treat as the acclaimed Miss Gertrude Challenger is billed to perform.

Into the 1930s now and we will wend our way down Westbourne Road and Belton Road and turn into Chaplin Road. We pass the Shepherds Rest which, thankfully, still stands today as 'Tony and Pam's'.

In Chaplin Road more VE Day festivities in progress in 1945.

A leap forward to 1953 as we look up Nicholas Road and catch up with the Benson family and their neighbours on Coronation Day.

One of the Bensons – Mike – stands to the right of the Lord Mayor with his friend, Ivor Blake. They are witnessing a presentation to local boy, Charlie Nicholls.

Walking briskly up Lawrence Avenue, we encounter Molly Maby's dog outside her house, No. 18. On the Rene Road corner can be seen Mrs Bolt's shop, one of many corner shops lost to us since the advent of supermarkets squeezed the small trader out of business.

As we re-emerge into St Mark's Road in the 1970s, Mrs Smeaton's grocery store is still in evidence on the corner of St Mark's Terrace. Her brother, Cliff Cannock, might be weighing up some Sturmers [New Zealand apples] two doors down. Opposite, John Perkins & Sons would still be hard at work in their shop-fitting business built around the remains of the Manor House.

St Mark's Road in the 1980s, showing the Perkins' building, left, middle distance.

Prior to its occupation by the Perkins Corporation, the old Manor House was used by a branch of the YMCA and during the 1920s and 1930s was the hub of local activities since it possessed a fine gymnasium, billiard room, and concert hall. Here we see the dining room laid out for what was obviously a special function. My grandfather, Rupert Ellery, was the steward there and my grandmother, Jane Ellery, was usually called in to assist. She is pictured here, third from the left. In front of her stands her younger daughter, Iris, who loved to help. Sadly, Iris died, aged 11, a couple a years after this photograph was taken.

The YMCA had a fine cricket team. Here, in 1934, Lionel Ellery and a fellow player have been joined by some girls, probably roped in to make sandwiches.

The YMCA play Kingswood Training School, 26 August 1933. My three uncles are all in the picture: Denis (seated, far left), Lionel (centre, holding bat) and Don (the youngster in the front).

In need of refreshment? Just up in Belmont Street stood the South Wales Railway Tavern when the station still possessed its elegant Victoria waiting rooms. This picture dates from the 1940s before the house adjoining the pub, together with others in the rank, was demolished for some scheme which never came to fruition. The site is now covered by a small park. The hostelry itself has been boarded up for the past couple of years and is falling into disrepair.

The last days of our lovely vicarage, scene of so many wonderful garden parties. It was torn down in the early 1980s to make way for the construction of flats commissioned by the Churches Housing Association. Fortunately, the vicarage grounds have been preserved so the new site is quite an attractive one.

Before leaving, we must call in upon Mr and Mrs Evans who ran St Mark's Road garage for so many years. We catch them here standing on the steps of the adjoining 'Elm House' with their daughter May.

May Evans again, some years earlier, by the oil containers. The garage no longer serves petrol but is still operational as a repair workshop, now in the hands of Impy Jiha, who informs me that Elm House, one of the oldest surviving properties in the area, was once used as a shoe factory. It is very gratifying to me that so many relative newcomers to the district, many originally from faraway lands, have such a deep interest in the locality's history.

Four
Baptist Mills to Stapleton Road

The unique character of this portion of Easton was completely annihilated during the late 1960s and the early 1970s. Gone are the cobbled streets, the quaintly shaped buildings and old pubs with names like 'The Artisan Tavern'. This was one of the earliest parts of Easton to be developed industrially owing to its proximity to the River Frome. The mills were hydro-powered and their products transported by boat. It must have been a bustling place during the eighteenth century when the pleasure gardens behind the Three Blackbirds inn reached down to the water's edge.

We'll take a last look up Stapleton Road towards Oxford Place, which is our next destination, and see the elegant shops in their heyday. This section of the road was built in the late 1880s. Prior to that the land had been given over to market gardens and, as late as 1882, when the houses facing were well established, as was the left-hand side of Seymour Road, this piece of ground is marked 'Nursery' on the map of that year.

So on to Oxford Place, where we find a party setting off on a charabanc outing in the 1920s. They are leaving from the Victoria on the corner of Blenheim Street. It can be observed that hats were de rigeur in those days.

From 1935 until the mid-1950s the landlord of the Victoria was Harry Bray who is seen here looking from an upstairs window. The Mill House sheltered accommodation now stands on this spot. Half of Blenheim Street and all the properties from the corner of Oxford Place, where a fish shop stood next to the Duke of Cambridge (which was spared), were demolished for this project.

A very definite Victorian ambience about this view of Walpole Street in the 1950s. Mollie Ward and companion show off their fancy dress costumes.

Mollie and her friends play near her house. Our mothers even dressed us up to go out to play in those days, didn't they? Perhaps they thought we wouldn't play such rough games if we were wearing frocks. Maybe they were right.

Baptist Mills School has now been drastically altered and renamed Mill Pond Primary. Once it huddled hidden behind a row of dwellings, shops, pubs, and a chapel which comprised a section of Lower Ashley Road. This entire terrace was swept away to make way for school playing fields. Here we find some pupils from 1907 looking very smart and well scrubbed. Some of the boys are wearing medals. Could they have been won by their fathers in the Boer War, I wonder?

Baptist Mills School in the 1930s, with pupils tending the spring floral display. Among them is Audrey James who grew up to marry into the well-known Cook family who owned fish shops in Oxford Place and Stapleton Road.

Audrey and her classmates again – this time celebrating May Day. Audrey is in the middle, at the front.

To the Swinging Sixties now and spirits are high on leaving day. These two pictures are of Jenny Worgan and her pals but neither she nor I can puzzle out the street sign on the house at the rear. It surely ought to be Millpond Street but it looks to be a shorter word.

Another group sampling the heady anticipation of starting work. A preponderance of pencil skirts with kick pleats at the back is in evidence.

A more sober collection with one girl at least sporting a paper nylon underskirt. We kept them stiff by washing them in a sugar solution!

A few boys have been lured into the picture, with a James Dean clone on the far left.

At the top of Claremont Street, the church now used by the Greek Orthodox congregation was once known as St Simon's. The spire has recently been altered. Here we happen upon a Coronation Day party in the church hall (*above*) and the fancy dress parade (*below*).

The following two photographs are thought to be of St Simon's School. In the first, we see the older girls, most in their crisp white pinafores to keep their clothes clean (no easy-care fabrics in those days!).

In this photograph the children seem to be holding up pictures, perhaps commemorative portraits depicting the coronation of George V? One girl in the front is holding a baby and another at the back is in charge of a toddler.

As we make our way down Claremont Street, we will rest for a moment in Bean Street, vestiges of which can be still be seen behind the church. This thoroughfare led down into Pennywell Road and it was here, in 1913, that Ted Palmer was apprehended and charged with the murder of his fiancée, Ada James. He was found guilty and hanged. Here we catch the children of Bean Street posing for the camera. Just look at those collars! The boy on the window sill is clearly a lad prone to bronchial infections judging by the king-size muffler wrapped around his neck!

Entitled 'Smith's Outing', this postcard depicts residents setting off on a trip in July 1920 and also another splendid array of hats. The boy in the right-hand corner looks as though he is encased in a dustbin or boiler.

Children line up beside St Simon's Church on Pound Day – a yearly ritual – 1930s. Every child had to bring a pound of some provision – be it sugar, flour, currants, or any ingredient which could be used to bake bread, cakes, or pies for distribution amongst the needy of the parish.

Mrs Hilda Tregaskis, pictured outside her Bean Street home with her dog. Just look at those beautiful lace curtains and the fringed roller blind!

The land between Claremont Street and Seymour Road was cleared in the 1960s and the Charlotte Keel Health Centre was built. Here Sister Jaycock (left) smiles in the way she did just before administering a Jectofer [iron injection for anaemic pregnant women] jab!

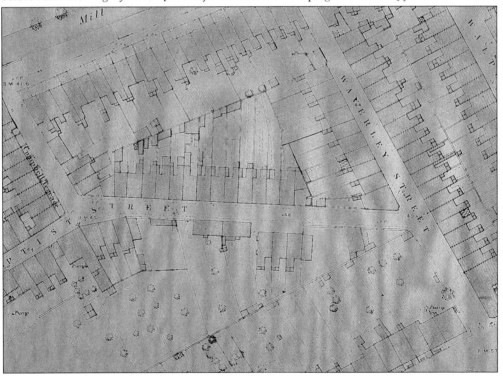

If we continue down Claremont Street, the next turning on the right would have been Amberley Street, which joined up with Beaumont Street at the Pennywell Road end. This picture would seem to date from the 1940s when the United Beers licensee was Herbert Eatell.

We pass Bedford Street and arrive at Russell Street which connected at the other end with Goodhind Street. On the corner stands the lead-windowed Claremont Tavern, the foundations of which now lie buried beneath Easton Way.

The section of Goodhind Street designated for redevelopment starts to fall. We call at No. 27 and sympathise with the occupant battling against the dust when trying to dry her washing.

Five

Stapleton Road

From before the late nineteenth century up until to the 1960s, Stapleton Road was one of the most varied and interesting shopping thoroughfares in the city, rivalled only, perhaps, by Gloucester Road. It contained a plethora of pubs, businesses, and shops, with fierce competition keeping prices down. It even possessed its own departmental store – Jones's – with an upstairs restaurant where weary shoppers could relax and gaze out at the activity in the street below (if you were fortunate enough to grab a window seat). Meals there were cheap and nutritious – my particular favourite was rissoles and mash with thick gravy, followed by prunes and custard. About 1950 this would have cost two shillings and threepence, including a cup of tea.

Pre-1960s, on leaving Claremont Street, you would have passed the doctor's huge house with its blocked-in windows (legacy of the old window tax when people bricked up rather than paying up!) and then on past a rank of shops which included a draper's, two milliners, a fishmonger, a butcher, and a grocery store. Altogether there were seventeen properties demolished in the 1970s to build the park which fronts Rawnsley House. It was at this time that half Beaumont Street was razed to rubble.

Our first port of call is the Armoury which, here in the 1940s, displayed an opulent tiled exterior, pride of the landlord, Joseph Leonard. From Reakes, next door, floated the glorious aroma of baked ham and faggots.

On the other corner of Armoury Square stood the Post Office Tavern, probably dating from *c.* 1908. Here an all-male party is about to embark on a day out, the cautious ones carrying mackintoshes and the devil-may-care brigade sporting boaters and tweed jackets.

The 1940s now, and gone are the luxuriant window boxes and the 'Old and Mild Beers'. In the 1960s the Post Office Tavern was converted into a butchers shop run by Mr Pegler. It survived a while after his death but is now empty.

As we walk on up the road in October 1972 we find that Jenny Worgan, whom we last met gleefully ending her academic career at Baptist Mills, has just married Reg Bell at the Congregational Church. This is a proof from their wedding photographs.

A few steps up the road bring us to the Sea Horse, now known as the White Elephant. The houses in Winsford Street were removed in the early 1970s for the construction of the new St Nicholas RC Primary School. On the right can be seen Buss's original greengrocer's, a tiny dark shop which they occupied before moving to the former premises of Strode, Cosh, and Penfold (chemists), at the top of Clark Street.

Another street now covered by the new school was Edward Place. The Royal Oak stood at the Pennywell Road end.

The Pennywell Road view of St Nicholas of Tolentine church when it was first opened in 1895.

We have arrived at Trinity Church now in time to see one of their football teams from the 1930s prepare to do battle against the opposition.

Another time, another team – forward to the 1950s and the Stapleton Road Youth team look pretty confident.

We return on the other side of the road, past a very spruce-looking Stapleton Road Tavern viewed from the corner of Harleston Street where Mr Constance once had his dental practice. Next door, Brown's occupies the building which is now home to Au Temps Perdu.

This side of Stapleton Road (c. 1958) would be unrecognisable to anyone who hadn't visited since the mid-1960s. How many people recall the Sadler's Arms? It was tucked on the corner of the Paddock next to RCA Motors (who used to display a magnificent vintage Austin 7 on their roof – how I coveted that car!).

We'll move on now past Thrissell Street
and Stanley Street with its narrow arched
entrance, trying to recall the scene before
the leisure centre was built. Here is
something to jog the memory – Beaufort
Street on a warm May day in 1965, with
Bird Lane running off on the right up to
Easton Road. Its days are numbered as
the ominous sight of the tower block
looming in the background forewarns.

A rainy day and, judging by the closed
doors of the Waggon & Horses, too early
for a warming dram. We remain in the
era of George's Brewery and the Diadem
Flour Company is still trading next door.
In the 1880s a brewery was situated
behind the pub.

Sister Louise (a nun from a local convent) actually ran a baby clinic in a back room of the Waggon and Horses. She was very persuasive when it came to raising money to help the children and would wheedle goods from local shopkeepers to use as raffle prizes.

A mystery now for eagle-eyed readers. This interior is believed to be of a local hostelry in the late 1930s. I am fairly certain it is the Waggon & Horses, although other suggestions have included the Black Swan.

Back again to the turn of the century to bid the patrons of the Alma Tavern a safe journey. I wonder whether the horses were provided by A.W. Grove?

Rogers & Son, dyers and cleaners, closed and awaiting demolition in 1967. This was No. 107 Stapleton Road, an area now covered by grass at the edge of the Twinnell House car park.

Glorious Grimsteads, which stood on the corner of Twinnell Road, seen here in the late 1930s.

The Little Victoria Street studio and we watch Daisy Luxton putting budding artistes through their paces. Here Audrey James and her fellow pierrots point elegant satin-encased toes for the benefit of the camera.

We remain in this little street (in the 1880s it was simply called 'Victoria Street') to join in the fun of the Coronation Day party in June 1953 which was organized by Rosa Brewer and her neighbours. Here Rosa herself, stands by the wall (second from right) flanked by her sister Margaret Williams and her friend Joyce Thatcher (née Gapper) on her left.

The girls again in attendance while the men sit down and tuck in. Rosa's husband Les is the one with the cheeky grin and the Bill Haley kiss-curl. The tables were set out in Little Albert Street.

Festive flags adorn No. 12. Mrs Foale sits on the wall while Rosa, Joyce, and Audrey Cooper (née Fear) pose outside Joyce's house. The children are Joyce's daughter, Cynthia, and Audrey's son Gerald.

The children wearing their party hats include Rosa's young brother, Robert Williams, sitting in the front row with his socks round his ankles. Betty and Eileen Waldron are in the back row.

The children march down the street. Outside No. 28, Rosa's house, stands her niece Christine attired as a mini bunny girl. The young man with the Tony Curtis hairdo is David Bennett.

Is Barry Gapper the winner by a short head? Or was he pipped to the post by Michael Brewer on the right?

Slipping back to 1927 we find the young residents of Little Victoria Street gathered outside the pub affectionately referred to as 'Aunties'.

Reg Brewer, the councillor who fought tooth and nail for the rights of the local people whose properties were under a compulsory purchase order. But for his efforts, even more of old Easton would have been wiped out and we would have lost the rank of shops stretching from Seymour Road to Oxford Place.

Six
St Gabriel's and Thereabouts

There was a veritable maze of streets between Stapleton Road and Easton Road prior to the large-scale demolition of the 1960s. As with most working class communities, it was a close-knit neighbourhood with families tending to live near one another – almost everyone had a relative living in the same street or else just round the corner so help was always at hand when a crisis arose. Many owners of small shops were compassionate when it came to matters of finance and were prepared to extend credit in genuine cases of hardship. Some would slip a little treat now and again to a needy child to alleviate the bleakness of its spartan existence.

It is the summer of 1953 as we pass through cobbled Gladstone Street to say 'hello' to residents off on a Coronation coach outing. Field View can now be found on this site.

Gladstone Street on VE Day. It was rare in those days to see the older generation of women without their pinnies.

The Gladstone Street party held to celebrate the coronation of George VI in 1937. Being May and the weather uncertain, these kiddies are in the hall of Gladstone Street Chapel.

Beaufort Street once more, this time looking down to Stapleton Road with the Mountstevens shop facing, a site from which they still trade thirty years on. The double-bayed houses on the right were constructed much later than the pre-1882 buildings on the left.

Cutting through Clifton Place brings us into Twinnell Road, now covered by Wills Drive, Durbin and Ashman Walks. In this view, from the 1960s, we look down to Clifton Place, with Eagle Street running off to the right, to link with Twinnell Street.

Parallel to Eagle Street ran Lion Street. St Gabriel's Road is in the distance.

Halfway up Lion Street we come to the Lion public house. Mrs Nash was the landlady when this shot was taken in the 1940s.

The pub in 1965 as demolition day draws ever closer. The house next door, No. 28, has already disappeared.

The well-polished interior of the Lion lounge in September 1966. Its time might be running out but standards still had to be maintained.

The next street up was Seal Street and from John Bennett's back bedroom window at No. 3 in the 1950s we gaze down and catch a glimpse of the large tree which grew in the Curnocks' garden in Upper Clifton Street – No. 29.

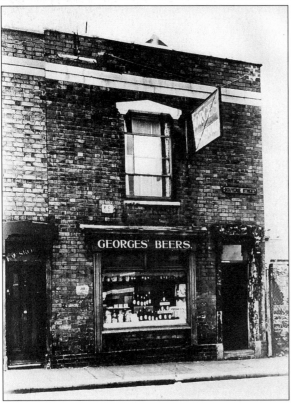

Crossing Twinnell Street we reach an unrecognisable Bouverie Street. This was the off-licence which stood on the corner. The Woods kept a shop four houses up from here.

Looking down Bouverie Street to St Gabriel's Church, May 1965. Some of the houses have already been pulled down for the building of Shaw Close and Abraham Close.

Emra House (later named Lansdowne Court to give it a better image!) in 1968, taking shape inexorably behind where Australia Place once stood. Only a matter of time now before the church and adjoining school follow suit.

The church was the setting for many weddings. I was bridesmaid there in 1945 when my uncle Don (Ellery) married auntie Kathleen. In this group Joan Lewis is the bride. Little Victoria Street is behind the churchyard wall.

Many will remember Revd Bulman seen here delivering his last sermon in the church…

Revd Bulman officiating at a wedding in the 1950s.

Still in the 1950s we meet the choir. The three girls at the back on the left-hand side are Mavis Hogan, Margaret Southron, and Monica Hogan, all school chums of mine, and the first two on the left in the front are Elaine Brown and Sylvia Bulman.

Many romances began at church in those lost days of innocent love. Here Charles Bulman, the vicar's son, marries Barbara Brown.

From high up in Rawnsley House can be viewed the new dwellings which rose from the ashes of Stork Street, the right-hand side of Bouverie Street, Seal Street, Lion Street, and Twinnell Street. The left-hand side of Bouverie Street has not yet been torn down and rebuilt and the church and school still stand. The Salvation Army Church will disappear by the mid-1970s, although the site remains undeveloped to this day.

Most of the local children attended St Gabriel's School. Class 3 are pictured here, *c.* 1910.

In the 1920s Jack Payne played the king in *Pictures from Storyland*.

More theatricals from the same era featured Les Brewer and classmates.

A more formal ensemble – class IVb at St Gabriel's Infants' School in 1925.

A well-scrubbed class 5 at St Gabriel's Boys' School in 1931.

An assortment of fashions – class 4 at St Gabriel's in 1933.

St Gabriel's Boys' School cricket team in 1933. Some jeering faces can be seen in the classroom window.

A cheery group from 1934 – class II at St Gabriel's Boys' School.

Some older boys from St Gabriel's, also from 1934.

Holding the slate in this photo from St Gabriel's Girls' School is Joan Lewis whom we encountered earlier in the section on her wedding day. Iris Mitchell sits nearest the camera and behind her Rose Carr looks rather impish.

Joan Lewis, by this time a prefect at St Gabriel's, stands to Mrs Tipper's right, while to the other side is Betty Martin, 1935.

Doreen Payne (later Howarth) sits in front, far right, with these other five-year-olds in 1936.

Up to 1946 now to see John Bennett and his classmates.

Miss Dudridge's class, 1950s.

Smiling sweetly for Mr Willis, mid-1950s.

Plaid was obviously in fashion during this year in the 1950s.

The older children at the front of the school, *c.* 1954. In the background can be seen the Gothic cottages.

Mr Colin Webb's class. From left to right, back row: John Cooper, Terry Withers, Malcolm Williams, Richard Moore, Paul Barnett, Paul Gillam, Christopher Kendall. Third row: Michael Lines, Brenda Payne, Lyn Langley, Janet Richard, Lyn Hunt, Josephine Garland, Sheila ?, Rita Gladstone, Yvonne Dyke, Susan Saunders, David West. Second row: Linda Morse, Pauline Downs, Valerie Burge, Pauline Moir, Heather Amery, Pauline Hallett, Deborah Cooper. Front row: Stephen Hooper, Gerald Batt, Ian Smith, Steven Vlad, Stuart Fellows, Paul Tweedle, David Kellard, Daryl Base.

To the church hall now where the Cubs and Brownies seem to be having a fine old time in 1951.

The Civil Defence faced an awesome task in Easton during the Blitz. Doll Batt, front row, third from left, displayed such valour in rescuing the survivors of bombing attacks in the area that she was awarded the George Cross and will never be forgotten by those who lived through those dark days. Ralph Robbins who loaned me the picture is far left, middle row. At the other end of this row are Jim Baker, a local coal merchant and next to him, Fred Bennett. It is thought that the Cunninghams, father and son, are in the back row, second and third from left.

Seven

Easton Road to Roman Road

There is nothing left of Easton Road and its surrounding streets as we once knew them. Designated 'slums', whole streets were wiped away and dozens of shops, businesses, and public houses were pulled down to be replaced by hideous tower blocks and maisonettes. The council pledged to build new schools, libraries, parks, and an up-to-date shopping precinct, but this proved to be an empty promise. The area's spirit lives on, however, as can be witnessed by the hundreds of people who flock back to the reunions organized by Mike Purnell. Let's look back to how it used to be.

Following our route from Bouverie Street we will first stop and see what Tovey's have on offer. The large cockles sound rather appetising.

Inside the shop a tray of winkles catches the eye and the 'Far-North' fish paste is a snip at only 1s 4d for three.

A few yards up the road we find ourselves back in the 1930s outside Batt's off-licence on the corner of Twinnell Street and Easton Road.

By 1966 disintegration has set in. There's an empty site where Batt's had so recently stood. Twinnell Street is disappearing and the Union Tavern looks lost and lonely.

Let's step inside the public bar and try to remember happier days.

Up the road a little way we pause at Easton Road School and watch the children play their last games there.

We look across the railings to a rapidly changing vista and catch echoes of children's voices from the past.

Here are some of these children: Jack Bryer, second from left in the back row, is surrounded by his friends from the 1935–36 class.

Out of school and on the rampage, c. 1950. From left to right, back: Michael Purnell, Ken Wall. Front: Colin Dickson, David House, Trevor Warden, Robert Backwell.

This well-behaved looking set of pupils at Easton Road Primary School *c.* 1950 includes Trina Pomphrey sitting at the back next to the boy in glasses.

Miss Marley's class at Easton Road Primary School, *c.* 1950. From left to right, back row: Francis Davis, David Caines, Jean Moore, Martyn Baldwin. Third row: Barry Hudson, Nyren Yeo, Marlene Wall, Sylvia Joyner. Second row: Arthur Savage, June Stone, David Tovey. Front row: Joy Street.

Hilda Pomphrey and her niece Jacqueline on a sunny day in Thrissell Street. It is the 1960s and bucket bags and bouffants are all the rage.

The last property in Easton Road undergoing renovations. In the 1940s auctioneers Chaucer Jewell and Co. traded from this address. Judging by a poster on the wall of Fox Terrace proclaiming the superiority of 'Tide', this photograph may well date from the 1950s.

The Three Tuns stood facing
Thrissell Street and was much
patronized by employees of the
engineering firm after which the
street was named. The Morris
Traveller in the foreground
suggests a date of about 1960 for
this photograph.

Next along was the Marlborough.
The licensee at this time was Doris
Hathway.

The smartly turned-out Easton Road Band played many a stirring march.

The YP String Band gather in Wellington Terrace, *c.* 1921. From left to right, back row: Mary Withey, -?-, -?-, -?-, Doris Perkins, Edna Hoare, -?-. Front row: Olive Short, -?-, -?-, Mrs Rossiter, Mr Rossiter (bandmaster), Capt. Bentley, Sgt. Major L. Aubrey, -?-, Mary Stabb.

1 Chaucer Jewell & Co. auctnrs. & valuers
3 Warfield B. & H. paint mers
5 & 5A, Warfield B. bldr. & decrtr
7 Lord Chancellor (Wm. Jn. Crotty)
9 Lines & Sons, cycle dlrs
11 Lines & Sons, tobccnsts
13 Easton Fish Saloon, fried fish dlrs
——*Paddock & Thrissell Sts. intersect*
25 Davies Rd. & Son, undertakers
25 Davies Wm. Hy
27 Parsons Fredk. Chas
29 Christenson Alfd
31 Potter Miss Kathln. coffee rms
33 Ellans Jn
35 Biddle Geo
37 Harvey Mrs
39 Parry Fredk
41 Cocks Mrs. Isabella
43 Rennolds Wm. R
——*Stanley Street intersects*
45 Royal Oak (Mrs. May G. L. Balson)
47 Alice's (Kerswell & Balchin), gown specialists
49 Holmes Chas
——*Bird Lane intersects*
51 Goding Ernest, confctnr
——*Hulbert Street intersects*
53 O'Brien T. Son & Allen, electricians
55 Down Ernest Albt. boot repr
COUNCIL SCHOOLS
57 King Miss Sarah

EASTON PLACE.
2 O'Brien Mrs. Clara
3 Davey Leonard Geo

59 M.C.B. Prams, perambulator reprs
59A, Ashby Percvl. Sidney
61 Earner Miss Alice
63 Dyer Philip Edwd
65 Humphries Fredk. Jn

69 Edbrooke Mrs. Gladys, butcher
——*Gladstone Street intersects*
73 Helps Bros. cabnt. mkrs
81 Bird Mrs. Sarah
81A, Britton Albt
83A, Crewe Fredk. Albt
85 Williams J. & Sons, bedding & mattress mkrs
87 Union Tavern (Wm. Jas. Couch)
——*Twinnell Street intersects*
89 Batt Mrs. Lucy Amelia, beer retlr. (off)
91 Stabb Mrs. Mary
93 Greenhalgh Wilfred, pianoforte dlr
95 Howe Mrs. Elsie, greengro
97 Britt Jn. Wm
99 Wools Mrs. Rose
101 Williams Jas. Jsph
103 Hudson Mrs. Maria
107 Marise (Mrs. Anne Gurney, proprietress), ladies' hairdrssrs
109 Adams Arth. Fredk
111 Tovey Wm. fishmngr
113 Darnley Mrs. Phyllis, draper
115 Nichols Herbt. confctnr
117 Coster Miss Laura
119 Cave Victor
121 Raffill Alfd
123 The Talbot (Mrs. Rose Eliz. Trott)
127 Starr Gilbt
129 Walker Geo. Stephen
131 Perrett Ernest Edwd
133 Fellows Frank
135 Furlong Martin
137 Calvey Wm. Jn. Stickler
139 Brain David Chas. tailor
141 Passmore Mrs. Beatrice, furniture dlr
145 Faithfull Bros. Ltd. motor haulage contrctrs
147 Faithfull Bros. motor garage
——*Twinnell Road intersects*
167 Glue Geo. confctnr
——*Bouverie Street, John Street & Bannerman Road intersect*
171 Queen's Head (Geo. Wm. Winter)
173 Wilkins Arth
177 TOWN SUB-POST & M. O. OFFICE
177 Hall Fredk. Jas. statnr. & sub-postmaster
181 Smith Rt. & Son, bakers
183 Willcox Saml. Chas. fried fish dlr
185 & 187 Hill Sidney
——*Wright Place intersects*
191 Leigh Herbt. cooked meat dlr
193 Mills Mrs. Winifred H. tobccnst
195 Lewis Herbt. locksmith
197 Ellis Wltr. pork butcher
199 Hit or Miss (Geo. Perry)
——*All Hallows Road intersects*
201 Stone Sidney
201 Lawrence Panel Beating Co. (The), panel beaters
203 Osborne Fras. Hy
205 Clark Percy Wm
207 Jones Arth. Saml
209 Rays Jn
211 Fox Wm. Berkeley
213 Tyler Frank
215 Mass Geo. Sydney Hugh
——*Brighton Park intersects*
219 Jefferies Albt. Jas
221 Curnock Wm
221 Curnock G. & Sons, plasterers

——*Raburn Street intersects here cross over*
254 Britnell Geo
252 Hill Ernest Geo
250 Bourne Ernest Jn
248 Bourne Edgar
246 Mullins Jn
——*Windsor Grove intersects*
242 Jenkins Clifford Jn
240 Hayers Thos
238 Cozens Mrs. Nellie
236 Tranter Wm. Chas
234 Fletcher Regnld. Vivian
232 Bath Chas. Hy
230 Baker Misses Lilian & Eliz
228 Benger Mrs. Maud
226 Griffee Mrs. Bridget May
224 Godfrey Alfd. plasterer
222 Lewis Geo
220 Linton Mrs. Ada
218 Hibbs Thos. Fredk
216 Carter Mrs
214 Walker Jsph. Wm
212 Hall Wm
——*Brixton Road intersects*
208 Pearce Ernest, shopkpr
206 Fretwell Jn. ironmngr
——*Tyndall Road intersects*
204 New Inn (Mrs. Alice A. Bennett)
202 Small L. & Son, greengros

200 Roberts Fredk
198 Chapman Ernest Edwd
196 Jenkins —
194 Tanner Geo
192 Bray Fredk. boot repr
186 Roberts Mrs. Gladys May
184 Tamlyn Geo. Harvey
METHODIST CHURCH
168 Huntley Victor T. motor engnr
168 Silver Sails (Bristol) Ltd. taxi-cab proprs
Bristol Tramways & Carriage Co. Ltd. (The), garage
150 Davidson Rev. Stanley Guest (priest in charge of St. Lawrence)
148 Evans Herbt. Jn
146 Hall Frank Danl
144 Salvation Army Officers' Quarters
142 Parsons —
140 Howard Mrs. Mercy Annie
138 Stallard Ernest
136 Hemmings Saml
134 White Miss Dorothy Lucy
132 Tambling Wltr. Herbt
130 Lovell Wilfred Chas
126 Wallace Edwd
124 Pritchard Chas. Hy
122 Fowler Chas. Wm
120 Standerwick Edwd
118 Brice Jn
116 Bindon Mrs. Ellen, genl. dlr
——*Croydon Street intersects*
114 Clements Thos. newsagt
112 Hampson Mrs. Alice
110 Gingell Wm. Jas
108 Dyte Edwd. Alfd
106 Veals Rt
104 Jasper Leonard
102 Thompson Bros. hay & straw dlrs
——*Leadhouse Road intersects*
100 Paxton Arms (Thos. Rd. Scott)
98 Sullivan Edwd. Jn. oyster bar
96 Jarrett Dennis, hairdrssr
94 Macey Raymond Frank
94 Johnson Miss Annie
92 Parry Wm
90 Sherwood Hy
88 Hope Roy, fried fish dlr
86 Llewellyn Wm. Aubur-, booksllr
84 Stiles Edwin Geo. cooked meat dlr
82 Howe —
80 Brett Leonard S. pawnbroker
78 Berry Chas
74 Roberts Geo. greengro
——*Park Street intersects*
70 Allwood Ernest Stephen, baker
68 Jubb Mrs. Edith
66 Wathen Albt
64 Baker Mrs. Florence, draper
62 Howe Mrs. Rosina, shopkpr
60 Albion (Mrs. Ada Amelia Rodbourn)
——*Leigh Street intersects*
58 Rixon Wm. & Son, boot & shoe dlrs
56 Lingard Mrs. Florence Clara
54 Davis Wm
52 Chapman Jn
50 Ash Mrs. Florence Elsie
48 Flare Jn. Campbell, shopkpr
——*Wellington Street intersects*
46 Robinson Albt. shopkpr
42 Rowe Edwd. Jn. boot repr
SALVATION ARMY HALL
40 Ball Alfd. hairdrssr
38 Little Chas
36 Dudbridge Fredk
34 Helps Albt. Edwd. grocer
32 Davies Mrs. Louisa
30 Lines Edwd. C
30 Lines & Sons, haulage contrctrs
28 Marlborough (Lilian Doris Reed)
26 Ford Kestor Jn
22 Three Tuns (Mrs. Ellen Gertrude Harris)

A page from the *Kelly's Directory* of 1947.

The place, Fleet Street, the year, 1937 – coronation year for George VI. Fleet Street was a little cul-de-sac off Leadhouse Road, now interred somewhere beneath Paynes Drive. George Wall is the little boy, third along from the front, facing the camera. Among the women present are Mrs Long, Mrs Clements, Mrs Studley, and Peggy Plenty.

Another turning off Leadhouse Road was Park Row. This is the view outside the New Inn when it was run by Mr and Mrs Stubbins. Their dog is in the centre of the picture.

We are the champions! Celebration night at the New Inn for the successful darts team. Mrs Stubbins is bottom, far left.

Mr Stubbins (centre) prepares to set out on a coach trip with some of the regulars.

Croydon Street joined up with Leadhouse Road at the Lawrence Hill end and this whole compact little area was almost like a village. As we join in the high jinks at this 1953 coronation party in Leadhouse Road, we find plenty of the Croydon Street crowd intermingling. Among the revellers are Mrs Purnell, Mrs Harris, Mrs Joyner, Mrs Houselander, Mrs Gardner, and Mrs Gaydon.

A laden table awaits the younger members of the party.

And the adults fortify themselves with something a bit stronger than lemonade.

Hilda Pomphrey again, dressed this time as a minstrel, in a fancy dress parade on a bomb site at the top of Leadhouse Road

A Croydon Street get-together from the 1950s held in Stapleton Road Congregational Church Hall. Among the crowd can be spotted Ronnie Lewis, Colin Little, Des Hunt, John Stone, and Gordon Thatcher.

Croydon Street itself, looking towards Lawrence Hill, 1960s.

Berkeley Street converged with Leadhouse Road at Lawrence Hill. Mr Harvey's hairdressing establishment can be seen in the background of this shot of the Rose off-licence in the late 1950s.

Croydon Street children, 1950s. From left to right: Ronnie Joyner, Stanley ('Chickie') Hemmings, David House, and Trevor Warden.

A solitary survivor, for a few months more at least, in the decimated Easton Road of 1965.

Down now to the Whitehall end of Easton Road for a retrospective view of one pub which was spared – the Queen's Head. The building next door was the post office, demolished to build a garage in the late 1960s.

Another New Inn – this one stood on the corner of Tyndall Road, now the site of 'Iceland'.

A last glance up Easton Road before we embark on the final leg of our journey. Some of these properties still stand today although those nearest the camera have been replaced by modern housing.

We turn off by the Plough into Kilburn Street. Today only the pub remains out of all these buildings photographed in the 1940s.

No. 14 Kilburn Street then home to the Irwin family, 1920s. Here we meet Norman, his brother Ron, and sister Enid. Norman now lives in Australia but retains a keen interest in the district.

A group of people in Kilburn Street who seem to be either campaigning or perhaps making some contribution to the war effort.

Owen Street Mission in 1947. From left to right, back row: Mr Benger, Mr Laney, Mr Brown, Mr Kingston, Mrs Brown -?-. Fourth row: -?-, Iris Bale, -?-, Miss Thompson, Mrs Kingston, Joan Smith, Rose Cambridge. Third row: Glenys Downs, Irene Brown, -?-, Margaret Perrin, Maureen Smith, Gilbert Cambridge, Brenda Burden, Reg Laney, Pat White. Second row: John Groves, John Thompson, David Benger, -?-. Front row: Iris Perrin (standing); Colin Downs, Graham Benger, Bobby Jones, Billy Hancock, John Hacker, -?-, ? Smith, Yvonne Deetmer, Joan Swinford, -?-, -?-.

The 24th Company (Owen Street) of the Boys' Brigade at Weymouth Camp, 1951. From left to right (standing): Graham Benger, Len Brown, Joe Brown, Colin Downs, Jimmy Brain. Kneeling: Brian Petty and Colston Dunn.

Owen Street Boys' Brigade, 1953. From left to right: -?-, Norman Shehean, Mike Nelmes, John Hacker, Tony Reynolds, John Tutty (officer), -?-, Ian Ball, ? Hembrow, Billy Hancock. Middle row: Brian Eley, Roland Hartell, Bobby Jones, Den Ley (officer), Percy Brown (captain), Colin Downs, Mike Chaffey, Brian Gingell. Front row: -?-, -?-, -?-, David Pine, Ian Passmore, ? Ayres, -?-, -?-.

Clarence House, before it became simply 'The Clarence', 1950s. The side windows are now bricked up.

On this sunny 1950s day we walk up Bloy Street, one of the first to be built in the sector, and pause at the off-licence on the King Street corner, then run by Charles Stedman. By the time you read this, Bloy Street, as we knew it, will be changed beyond recognition since the houses have been deemed too expensive to repair and new dwellings are set to line the street.

Back to 1945 again to join in the fun at the Battersea Road VE Day party. The boys at the back are Brian Jones, Mike Powell, Brian Wright, Colin Downs, Brian Clayfield, and David Norton (?). In the middle are Maureen Bisdee, Barbara Greville, Brenda Smith, Olive Wiltshire (holding the baby), and Barbara Exon. The only identifications which can be made in the front are Ian Dury (on the left) and Maureen Smith (far right).

Map of the area in 1882.

We end our journey in Roman Road with a nostalgic look at the old Co-op building before the fire in the 1980s which destroyed the beautiful clock and the remains of the lettering which once proclaimed it to be the 'Co-op Laundry'.

I hope the excursion has not tired you too much, that you have enjoyed meeting old friends and revisiting long-lost locations and that some happy memories have been rekindled along the way.

CHELMSFORD WALK, St. Anne's
Park (4). 62 St. David's crescent.
(No thoroughfare.)

1 Coffin Wm. Jn
3 Risdale Chas
5 Vincent Jas

7 Church Wm. Hy
9 Caswell Thos. Geo
11 Dancy Hy
13 Morgan Hy. Chas
15 Webb Regnld
16 Sedley Hy. Rd
14 Taylor Thos. Fras
12 Smith Ernest Fredk
10 Payne Morley Jsph
8 Fortune Wm. Jn
6 Daveridge Wm. Edwd. Geo
4 Buckle Wm
2 Hole Geo. Jas

CHELSEA PARK, Lower Easton (5).
26 Chelsea road.
(No thoroughfare.)

1 Davies Mrs. Ethel
3 Barber Thos. Hy
5 Radford Hy. Jesse
7 Sullivan Danl
9 Bury Jsph
11 Pearce Fredk. Hy
13 Powlesland Herbt
15 Scrase Saml. Albt
17 Miller Geo
19 Norton Miss Lilian
21 Sevier Thos
23 Hulbert Harold Edwd
25 Veal Thos. Fras
27 Beake Mrs. Charlotte
29 Jay Arth
31 Norman Wm. Geo
33 Brain Geo. Herbt
35 Pyne Leonard
37 Allen Norman
39 Peacock Gilbt
39 Clode Wm
41 Selway Mrs. Mary
43 Stone Frank
45 Seaborne Fredk. Fras
47 Greenland Mrs. Rhoda
49 Tucker Thos
51 Mason Fredk. Jn
53 Bowden Gilbt
55 Batt Hy. Chas. Thos
57 Creedy Mrs. Julia
59 Dix Miss Catherine
61 Baker Arth. Jn
63 Wright Albt
65 Lovell Edwd
67 Bath Geo. Ernest
69 Cottey Mrs. Annie
71 Groves Fras. Wm
73 White Mrs. Minnie
75 Catley Harold Regnld
77 O'Leary Jn
79 Tester Albt
81 Ashman Geo
83 Holland Mrs. Ruth
85 Prewett Chas. Edwd
87 Merchant Fras. Hy
89 Moult Fras. Alex
91 Adams Edwd
93 Stedman Page
95 Lyons Jas
97 Shehean Wltr. Louis
here cross over
104 Hodges Jn
102 Burr Mrs. Lucy Eliz
100 Yearsley Saml
98 Bennett Ronald
96 Chalmers Jn. Jas
94 Rogers Rt. Wm
92 Simpkins Mrs. Ellen
90 Hendy Edwd
88 Lewis Jas. Geo. Jsph. N.A.M.H.
    herbalist
86 Newman Hy. Geo
84 Jarvis Mrs. Isabella
82 Hill Mrs. Ethel
80 Durbin Mrs. Ada
78 Gosling Edgar Woodward
76 Slocombe Jas
74 Burton Herbt
72 Langley Wilfred, boot repr
——*King Street intersects*
70 Hodges Mrs. Rose Colston
68 Gomm Wm
66 Smith Wm. Jn. haulage contrctr
64 Catley Leslie
62 Down Miss Caroline
60 Howard Wm
58 Rugg Mrs. Rosa Henrietta
56 Willmott Christphr
54 Chappell Cyril Sinclair
46 Martin Fredk
44 Lott Fredk
42 Westaway Jn
40 Bloomfield Chas
38 Harper Hy. Geo
36 Lewis Miss Florence Ada

34 Holley Saml
32 Takle Wm
30 England Mrs. Edith
28 Blake Regnld. Wm
26 Tidball Wltr
24 Hodges Saml. David
22 Roberts Mrs. Louisa
20 Bowden Leslie Fredk. Geo
18 Monks Fredk
16 Perham Mrs. Emma
14 Pope Sidney Victor
12 Harris Herbt
10 Clark Arth. Ernest
8 Potter Wm
6 Clarke Arth. W
4 Dymock Mrs. Sarah
2 Robbins Harold Cecil Wallace

CHELSEA ROAD, Lower Easton (5).
Owen street to Lena street.

1 Norman Rt. Harry
5 Seymour Wm
7 Marsh Fredk. Jas. boot repr
9 Whitelock Hy. Wltr
11 Lloyd Wm
13 Stone Edmnd. draper
15 Hallett Leonard Arth
17 Yeandel Arth. G
19 Derrick Arth. Edwd
21 Sparrow Harry
23 Miller Mrs. Louisa
25 Iles Fredk
27 Bennett Jsph
29 Townsend Chas
31 Hodges Miss Eliz. Ann
33 Allen Edwd. Jas
35 Collins Misses Tilly & Nelly
37 Birch Mrs. Eva
39 Wallington Alfd. Jas
41 Maby Mrs. Rose
41 Hancock Wm. Jn
43 Holsgrove Wltr. Geo
45 Greenland Bert
47 Jefferies Mrs. Minnie
49 Paul Fredk. Wm. dairyman
51 Challenger Mrs. Charlotte
53 Harding Alex
55 Farrow Sydney Alfd
57 Silcocks Mrs. Eleanor
59 Arbury Mrs. Mary Eliz
61 Iles Mrs. Alice
63 Price Mrs. Florence
65 Stone Saml
67 Frampton Mrs. Agnes
69 Morgan Chas. Patrick
71 Shallard Mrs. Minnie
73 Allpass Alfd. Hy
75 Wilkes Clifford
77 Studley Miss Florence
79 Hobbs Hy. Jn
81 Stanwell Wood Products Ltd,
    domestic appliance mfrs
83 Studley Fras. Ewart
85 Yearsley Hy
87 Brown Frank Ernest, fried fish dlr
89 Howes Mrs. Clara
91 Howes Denis, newsagt
93 Cunningham Mrs
93 Charrett & Edwards, butchers
95 Harris Archbld. shopkpr
97 Dymmock Isaac
99 Jakaway Mrs. Winifred
101 Grist Frank R
103 O'Sullivan Mrs. Doris Edith
105 Bryant Mrs. Eliza
107 Wilson Jas
109 Skinner Mrs. Eliz
111 Parsons Chas. E
113 Harris Herbt. Jn
115 Dyer Miss Minnie
117 Wood Herbt. hairdrssr
here cross over
100 Marley Jn. Hy
98 Fitzgerald Jas
96 Duffner Fredk. E
94 Williams Miss Violet
92 Swain Thos. W
90 Harris Albt
88 Withington Mrs. Elsie, grocer
——*Britannia Road intersects*
76 Thorne Jn
74 Bird Mrs. Emily
70 Collins Mrs. Ann
68 Harris Chas
66 Westmacott Miss Frances M
64 Batt Hy. Albt. greengro
——*Bloy Street intersects*
60 & 62 Clarence House (Mrs. Lily
    Rosina Morgan)
58 Cook Fredk. Geo
56 Davies Alfd
54 Gill Mrs. Agnes
52 Dredge Harold
50 Harvey Ernest S
48 Bartlett & Owen, drapers
48 Sommerfield Stanley
46 Feaver E. Jackson, chemist
44 Bristol Co-operative Society Ltd
——*Colston Road intersects*

40 & 42 Bristol Co-operative Society
    Limited
38 Bryant Leonard, hardware dlr
36 Chappell Fred Harvey, shopkpr
34 Saunders Rd. newsagt
32 Smart Alfd. butcher
32 Long Jas. Gilbt
30 Tyler Arth. Hy. greengro
28 Howes Rowland, grocer
28 Town Sub-Post & M.O. Office
——*Chelsea Park intersects*
26 Sparkes Jn. Hy. David
24 Webb Mrs. Sophia, grocer
22 Bryant Wm
20 Wheeler Arth. Jn
18 Justin Claude Ernest
14 Lawrence Wm
12 Derrick Frank
——*Battersea Road intersects*
10 White Jas
8 Burden Chas
6 Burden Wm
4 Perrin Redvers
2 Lewis Fredk

CHELTENHAM ROAD (6). *Stokes*
Croft to Gloucester road.

127 Cole Wm. B. jun. canine specialist
129 Price Edwd
131 Willmott Albt. E
133 Speller Chas
    The Academy Cinema (Atkinsons
    Pictures Ltd, proprs)
141 Powell Albt. Stanley
141 Coomber Mrs. M. E
143 Ellis Miss Gertrude, dressmkr
143 Joy Wm. Arth
143 Thompson Mrs
143 Kitchen Geo
145 Morris E. G. herbalist
147 Smith Mrs. Eliz. Josephine
149 Yentella Transport Café
151 Davies Cyril Ivor M.R.C.S.,
    L.R.C.P., L.D.S.R.C.S.Eng. dental
    surgn
153 Paradise Mrs. F. E
155 Huxtable Melvard, dentist
157 Bristol Insulation Co. (The), boiler
    & steam pipe coverers
157 Downey Peter
157 Cornish H
159 Allen Wm. Rt
161 Taylor D. carpet mer
163 Dark Rt. teacher of singing
165 Mahle Mrs. Annie
——*Arley Hill intersects*
    Arley Congregational Chapel
167 Potts Chas
167 Stafford Mrs. M
167 Reed Percy
169 Chamberlain Miss Phyllis
169 Puddy Mrs. Tabitha
169 Cox Miss Gladys
169a Croydon Misses
171 Fazel B. eye specialist
171a Jenner Wilfred
171b Leakey Miss E
173 Jones Mrs
175 Amos Alfd. Jn
177 Maddicks Misses
179 Jones Wilfred Grantley

    Llanarth Villas.
2 Capstick Alfd. Chas
2 Green Fredk
3 Thomas Miss
4 Williams Fredk. Regnld
5 Sainsbury Edwd. (Pastor)
5 Slater Norman Geo

185 Beavis Mrs. Ruby
187 Black Alex
187 Gillingham Wilfred

    Cheltenham Crescent.
1 Weeks Stanley
2 Perrett Jsph
3 Councell Mrs
4 Curthoys Alfd
5 Spencer Mrs. B
5 Cleaves Mrs. R
——*Winsley Road intersects*
    Bristol Public Libraries (North
    District Branch)
191 Harvey Mrs. Florence
193 Hutchison Harold W. T
——*Brookfield Road intersects*
195 Everest School of Commerce & Type-
    writing Office
195a Bagg Edwin Austin
195b Cole Dennis Ernest
195b Taylor Ronald
195b Tanner Ernest
195d George Mrs. Edith
197 Tanner Eric J., L.D.S. dental surgn
201 & 203 Fair S. J. Motors Ltd. motor
    car agts

A page from *Kelly's Directory*, 1947.

'Ghosts of Easton'

The coming of evening, diminishing daylight,
Strange shapes seem to glide from the gathering gloom;
Mysterious movements are sensed in the shadows,
I seem to hear whispers right here in my room

Remember the man said to be an old soldier,
The archway his shelter in sun and in rain?
Do I imagine harmonica music?
And is he still playing that plaintive refrain?